FINISHING LINE PRESS

www.finishinglinepress.com

LITTLE VICTORY

poems by

Elizabeth Kuelbs

Finishing Line Press
Georgetown, Kentucky

LITTLE VICTORY

for Sharon and Mike

ACKNOWLEDGMENTS

Many thanks to the editors who first selected these poems, sometimes in
different forms, for publication:

"Alis Grave Nil," and "Cut Your Baby Down," published as "What To Do
After Climate Week," *Poets Reading the News*
"Winter Bees," *The Timberline Review*
"Tender Grit," *Mothers Always Write*
"Little Victory," *The Ekphrastic Review*
"Bloom," *Kissing Dynamite*
"Hot Spring," Minerva Rising Press's *The Keeping Room*
"Bioluminescence," *The Poeming Pigeon*
"Celestial Fixer," *The Sunlight Press*
"Unsinkable Dogs," *Solo Novo 7/8: Psalms of Cinder & Silt* (Solo Press, 2019)
"West Coast Plover Power," *Poems for Plovers* (Hawk & Whippoorwill, 2020)
"Flower Moon," *Black Bough Poetry*

Publisher: Leah Huete de Maines
Editor: Christen Kincaid
Cover Art: Chloe Kuelbs
Author Photo: Betsy Newman
Cover Design: Elizabeth Maines McCleavy

Order online: www.finishinglinepress.com
also available on amazon.com

Author inquiries and mail orders:
Finishing Line Press
PO Box 1626
Georgetown, Kentucky 40324
USA

Table of Contents

Inspired by the tenet of chaos theory that small changes in initial conditions can spark great consequences, the poems in this collection call out dangers of denial in the seats of power and offer energy to face them by celebrating little victories of connection and wonderment.

Sangria

Despite the bristle-busting gusting and cruel
smoke smearing the dear moon, the witches
one by one alight upon the doorstep, and,
starved for sweet company, right their

hats before entering the candlelit party
to kiss hello and admire each other's elegant
capes and expertly kohled eyes. They sigh
down around the coffee table, shrug sick

children, mad kings, the charring heat
off their weary shoulders for one turn of
sand anyway, lamenting that their wands
are only plastic and their spells for mac

'n cheese, but oh the clink of iced sangria,
the ruby bloom of wine and oranges, how
it perfumes   how it eases
their parched throats
                        oh the moon—

bone-bright and howling through the ash-choked wind.

Alis Grave Nil

mango marigold tiger
        wings
distill sun   flower countries
        of wind
until the lightest riot
        constellates sacred firs

orange stars tremble needles
        wreathe puddles and pond edges
thrill busloads of your children
        and your impossible aunts

what do you love

        the administration
says bisect flyway and floodplain
        flatten them wall them dam them light them so stark
everything

        dies in the glare

what do you love

        the guardians
say plant slender-leaved milkweed
        grow goldenrod, lantana, purple sage
nurse forage and nectar
        everywhere you can

everyone can heal

        nothing is heavy

or shall we mourn our billion monarch
        ghosts, shall we end them all, one small form
after another, drifting

        and the tortoises, the horny toads, the indigo snakes,
the ocelots, the pygmy owls, the pronghorns—

        what do you love

walls or life.

Cut Your Baby Down

Hold your baby, the one you have,
or will have, or were, warm and sleeping

on your chest, her velvet head nestled
under your chin, smelling of milk.

What would you do to ban chlorpyrifos
from his blooming brain, sulfur dioxide

from their pink lungs, lead from her fresh
veins, pangs from his teaspoon stomach?

What would you do to save them from
Woolsey & Maria & Thomas, from cash

blindered liars tying stiff nooses out of
stilled currents and winds? What would

you do to cut your baby down from the
gallows, where she cries on a block of ice

beside whales, bees, sparrows, and corals,
sequoias, krill, and mangroves, all parching

in the winter sun. We will

do everything

right?

Chaos Theory

Up the scorched hill, up the worn path
through charred pines, stride the dragon's
brave pages. He waits for his page-of-the-day
at the cave's mouth, where his smoke
fogs the hole and his red fangs thrill.

They do not fear his fumes, the pages,
nor his gouts of flame, the storms he molts
when his gut bursts his skin, the quakes when
his wings twitch. His off-gas and rage slide
from their slick suits. And he starves,

that bag of burn. They know he dreams
of their gold plates piled high with crushed
throats. That he drools for their pangolin
wine, that he hums their tunes of caged
sobs, of sound bomb blasts in the sea.

The dragon eats all they bring, for such long
years. Now his walls pinch. His tail cramps
in the stone hole. A wild molt brews. His hot
bulk swells and craves. He juts his barbed
jaw out of his cave and eyes the wide sky,

where his wings might stretch. Then
up the slope climbs a fresh page. Sweet
page, he trips at the heat of red fangs.
He falls on his spine. He rips his slick
suit. His palms shake but he spills

no throats. At home, his small son waits.
He does not want to die on this hill.
The plates strain his wrists.
He lays them down
for the dragon, who flicks his night tongue

between them. A butterfly floats through
the smoke. Blue, iridescent,
flower-bound,
its legs crumbed
with pollen.

Winter Bees

When I go to the market for tape
I am very ostrich
      all pecky face
            long neck
                  fast legs—
it's January and this has been happening, not
to mention the feathers popping out of my skin,
the way sand tugs at my chin, my
hands blurring—
you know how those nuclear
buttons and government
shutdowns take a toll on
definitions?

In the market there is
a honeyman. I don't think
he will give me a sample, being
so ostrich, but he puts a full spoon in my
blurry fingers. It's from Canada, he says,
from happy bees and the clean red
clover close to their hives. It

makes my entire mouth sweet
a meadow hums in my eyes

in Canada, the honeyman says,
winter bees eat honey
to survive.

Tender Grit

My tiny wild daughter
refuses pink chalk

drawing sidewalk roses
holds no magic for her

not when a street puddle
brims with clouds and girl—

before I can stop her
she bends to meet them

dips her forehead and
rises grinning, forever

crowned in grit and sky.

triggered

after Don Jr.'s 1/4/20 Instagram post

it's a little extra awesome
Hillary jailed on his mag
jammed into his gun
her face and her cell loaded with his bullets
under his gleaming visor
because he slays beasts too
not just drawings of grandmothers
but threatened sheep
leopards
you should see that elephant's tail stump
his shining knife
in the other picture
with his ammo belt
and his great dead
wonder

pandemic dream

the rats get cocky
and somersault around
the silent park like they
own the woodchips and
the owls talon down
from the steeples

their wings stirring scents of
cumin and garlic and sourdough

the evening cooking softening
the blue screens and fears of
drowned lungs and it smells so
good and sounds so sad under the
full moon all the ladies liberty
from New York to Paragould to
Paris jump free from their pedestals
and boom out a few knee bends as their
torches spark and their crowns point
forward

they thunder on unstoppable
copper feet to open the cages and
lift the sick to the hospitals in
their cool patinaed arms

a small kind one finds my brother
on whatever street
      he is on

and when everyone is safe

they circle the clown king
a garden of uncompromising faces
and they raise their tiny and colossal
flames and in that clear warm
light

he sees
what he has done

What Would Lorca Do?

Frank.
My Eye.
Blue, flaming,
with pointy fingers and a
black-and-white checkered
apron tied halfway up his pupil.

He's been lounging on my couch, singeing
my upholstery, cackling, *it's a lockdown, baby.*
He's perfectly happy stuck inside, reflecting the
terrible counts at me.

Nothing gets past him these days.
No angel wants to scorch her wings of steel
on the likes of him. And why would any muse
break quarantine right now?

If I pick up a pen, he laughs.
Why embarrass yourself? he asks.

His voice. Pour lighter fluid on charcoal bricked
from middle school and zits. Strike a match.

So much for nails of artistic truth.
Well.
Whatever.

It's five o'clock in the afternoon.
I put on my red dress.

Toro, Frank, I say,
swishing the dark silk
as his flames
lick my arms.

Then we dance
by my open window
to the rattle of rusty
knives.

Little Victory

after "The Winged Victory of Samothrace" in the Louvre, and
Yves Klein's ultramarine "La Victoire de Samothrace"

I

    the quarry the marble the sweat
    the chisel the belly the feather

Nike's wings livened in the cold stone and her breasts thrust forward
and her right hand cupped her lips and her cry swelled triumph over
Samothrace and her shadow cheered the gods

II

    the pilgrims the winds the battles
    the cracks the falls the dirt the shards
    the shovels the waves the Louvre

Up Yves Klein floated, up quite neatly from the beach, up through the
azure haze, up above his Nice, where he, prince of the void, signed the
sunlit far side of the sky, only begrudging the soaring gulls the holes
they punched in his masterpiece

    the pigment the resin the foil
    the gold the rose the flame
    the ashes the sponge the bruise
    the Giottos the gut the katas the saints
    the leaps the pills the rocket the heart—

III

Greatest painter in the world, Monsieur Le Monochrome, it is he who stuck me on this spike! That *crétin*, with his babble of infinity and space, with his naked swaying models, his "living brushes"—oh, *vive la liberté* for them!—he left me here, headless, armless, footless, crusted in his eyeball-sucking color while my steadfast mother, so far away, longs ever for her severed limbs, shedding her sacred dust into gawping mouths. He would have spiked her if he could!

the bits the screens the power

Doesn't this beat watching SpongeBob, girls? Ooh, look at that little purple angel! Isn't she exquisite?
*

She's blue, Mom. And she's not an angel. See? She's Victory. On a stick. Which makes no sense. Or, wait, it does. It makes the same sense as me saving for Coachella and you not letting me go.
*

You never give up, do you, Pol? Someday I'll be dead and then you can go wherever you want. For now, you'll just have to suffer. Oh, my God, Thalia! Don't touch!
*

But Mama the angel wants me to pick her up.
*

Ma'am! Keep the child behind the rope.
*

She doesn't want you to pick her up, honey, she's plastic.
*

Plastique! Voilá le sublime. Gods, I want off this…this stick!
*

Mama, you need to look with your listening ears!
*

Ha, right on, Thals. I bet I can print her for you.
*

You can? With her head on? And arms? And feet? And rainbow
fingernails?
*

Yeah. Totally.
*

Oh là là, to have fingers! And rainbows! *Je t'en prie.*

IV

        the viewers   *the love*

          the blue
              the blue
                    the blue

Bloom

The leaf-gold wind willows Jenna's hair
into my cupcake gloss. I don't care because
she equals PanAm jets and tap shoes
and I equal geodes and (will secretly marry)
Shadowfax. We lift the canoe off its stand,
swing it toward the sun-dazzled lake,
try not to scythe
the coneflowers, obedient.

> *Steps that can be taken:*
> *Stock walleye to hunt crayfish and*
> *minnows and free little Daphnia to eat*
> *the blue algae blooms. Plant calico aster*
> *and fern in the watershed to filter*
> *phosphorus and deter invasive*
> *species. Do not babysit*
> *for the Harley dad.*

Mallards burst up quacking
at two boys,
walking the waterline,
tall, gilded.
The grass unroots
at a beryl gaze, the chlorine sheen,
the high shoulders.
The lake laps at the bow.
One says, *We think you're cute.*
One says, *We want you to suck our*

Carpet the bedroom floor
with wire hangers so you hear if
the fish eyes at the window
try to get in. Mark your exits. Learn
to injure. Avoid stairwells, ponytails,
deep thought. Fist your keys. Pack
a canteen. Raise your daughters to
fight and your son to be a good man.

The ducks turn rooster
and splash down: all claws,
red wattles and skin crowns.
Oh. My. God, Jenna says. *Get off her yard.*
We shove out through the weeds
and paddle toward the bright middle,
my meat hands electric,
trembling.

Miscarriage

In 2019, Georgia's governor signed a restrictive abortion law that threatened women who miscarry with the possibility of criminal investigation.

How would they
choose
which women
to interrogate
about their hollowing
wombs, their
empty arms? Would
they assess the particular scent
of uterine blood?
The flavor of tears?
The decibels of sobs?
The color of skin?
Where would they fire
their questions?
Into the silent ultrasound?
The cold emergency room?
The midnight bed? The echoing nursery?
The first shower
after the stars blacken?
Would they have pulled my mother
from tending my toddler
while I lay bleeding
to demand
had I been perfect in my gestating?
Who are *they* who desire
to interrogate?
May our answers
incinerate with fury.

Hot Spring

Sleepless Santa Ana

       hurls heat through

the tangerine tree's

       spider silk lace,

launching husks and threads,

       gritting leaves and eyes,

but not so thick to veil

       the baby's dream dawn

peaching and bluing

       above the ridge and

the tough-rooted tangerine

       sweetening its small suns.

Bioluminescence

It's sunset and days
        of sanitizing cracker boxes, of fearing drowned lungs,
before the fish wash up,
        so when the beaches open we champagne cork
into the car, follow
        the canyon west toward spring tides lavish with rainfed
algae, swell by red swell
        summoning. Bandanaed, barefoot,
we join,
        all of us strange wrack clumped
along the waterline,
        the damp sand delicious, the top halves of distanced faces,
the coral sky darkening,
        the microscopic sirens out there multiplying.
And the sun sinks.
        Wrack rises. Phones glow. Light begs light
from the abundance
        blooming in the black until the breakers crash

             neon blue

                    foam fire

and those single cells ignite
      wave after wave
          commanding *watch us*
           live.

Weights and Measures

*Tahlequah, the Salish Sea orca who carried her dead calf for 17
days in 2018, was pregnant again in 2020.*

On the scales of possibility hang two pans.
In one, Tahlequah swells with calf, her pod

deft around her in the cool jade depths,
their calls seeking swift chinooks, their catch

fueling songs, breaches, wild-hearted *aahs*,
while the fish they miss flash in the rivers,

nourish fir roots, loft eagle talons, grace
plates with savory meat.

> In the other, old dams hang, and crumbling
> concrete, barged wheat, hot stalled water,
>
> tube-flung salmon, turbine-ground smolts,
> plastic-marbled flesh, corrugated ribs, blinding
>
> ship din, and Tahlequah. She pushes
> her cold   newborn
>
> one thousand miles   seventeen
>
> days   keening hollows   through   straits

And above the pans, perched on the beam that suspends them,
a small gray American dipper. In its beak, a salmon egg, translucent
as invention, plucked from the rushing, undammed Elwha.

Tardigrada Talismana

It was only college. Not a hazmat disaster. Not war. But
the year was rabid so the daughter masked her delicate

face, and declining full PPE armor, passed airport security
with too many soft parts out, then vanished into the terminal.

The mother slow-stepped backward home, baked sugar,
butter, and ginger into cookies, swept a deft knife to ice them

as clovers and scarabs, a red *dala* horse, cobalt evil eyes. She
imagined the daughter's grin when she opened the box, but

the year was fanged and it wasn't enough. So the mother
carried an empty jar to the stream. She knelt at the mud edge,

sank the glass into the water, raked in five hundred million years
of life with her fingernails, then screwed the lid tight over

her catch: tiny water bears, moss piglets, indestructible
tardigrade survivors of geysers, glaciers, thirst, starvation,

radiation, lovers or no lovers, and quite possibly, should they
be tested, asteroid strikes, gamma-ray bursts, and the howling

void itself. The mother armored the jar in bubble wrap,
nestled it among her fragrant charms, and sent the box off.

Celestial Fixer

Some dog days Sirius scents Earth wanting
and waxing rascal he leaps the wall of his
bright palace to comet off astral flare,
through gas and void and dust,
binding particle and wave
into exuberant
spark

then new,
flesh and bone, he
big-bangs into the observable
universe, busts musty orbits with
the horizon of his gravitational coat,
the tidal loll of his tongue, the bold fusion
of his heart, eclipsing distance to draw palms

to fur, pulses to hum, star-stuff to star-stuff,
cosmically patient or piratic as required
to launch such fresh ellipticals.
Then he, job done, novas
home, leaving only
his glowing
tracks.

Unsinkable Dogs

In the back of my house the president brags
about marching 15,000 troops south to keep
out the 3,000 or 5,000 or infinite mothers and
fathers and children seeking refuge at our border.
If they throw rocks, he says, the rocks will
equal bullets and his soldiers will fire.

In the front of my house fairies and pumpkin
babies ring the doorbell. I kneel to offer chocolates.
Happy Halloween, I say, but what I mean is, please
be safe, because gusts singe their wings and
everything we've been feeding the wind heats its hunger
until it bites with teeth the size of the sky—

Bullets murder dancers and heroes at the Borderline.
Mountains ignite. Smoke eats the sun.
Flames raven, insatiable, incinerating lions,
canyons, houses, and we are all refugees

with no time to mourn in the raining embers
in the orange-lit parking lots and hotels where we tremble
where we cough ash, where we wipe it from our eyes

where our unsinkable dogs wag love
until we meet each other new
until the heroes douse the monsters

and we, kiln-fired, sleeves-rolled,
alive
grieve our ruins and our dead

and take note
of the tender green shoots
braving the scorched slopes.

West Coast Plover Power

You snowy little sand puffs
        little seize-the-days charging
                beaks open through swarming
kelp flies, broken-winging
        crows and skunks away from
                your bare buff eggs, or your
thumb-big chick puffs hiding flat until
        you win and snug them
                under your warm bellies
until the sun says dance up
        shrimp from the wave lips
                to skim the foam to outlast
the dogs and the joggers
        and the slicks and the cats—
                dance on you plucky little
toothpick-legged mamas and papas,
        we see you at Coal Oil Point,
                at Bolsa Chica, in Monterey,
we can see you, please
        dance the hell and the love on.

Flower Moon

Before dawn breaks
catch the palms:

those dutiful guards,
who shade their little

daytime queendoms
feeding bees and woodpeckers,

in the windy dark,
when the jacarandas

lavish blossoms at their
feet and the roses exhale

honey and clove,
and the jasmine

trembles like a bride,
and their lush plumes,

sequined with stars,
ravish the flower moon.

Additional Acknowledgments

I would like to thank Leah Maines and Christen Kincaid of Finishing Line Press for their supportive editorial guidance. Boundless gratitude to my dear friend and companion in poetry Laura Reece Hogan, and to my family, Brian, Michaela, Chloe, and Daniel, Polly and Jim, and Sharon and Mike, for their cherished inspiration and support. Gratitude also to Elizabeth Bradfield and Rachel Kann, whose amazing workshops led to some of the poems included in this book, and to Jason Gray for his encouragement. Finally, sincere thanks to Chloe Kuelbs for bringing the heart of this book to visual life with the cover art.

Elizabeth Kuelbs lives with her family at the edge of a Los Angeles canyon. A poet, writer, and former management consultant, she holds an MFA from the Vermont College of Fine Arts, and an MS in Information Systems Analysis and Design from the University of Wisconsin-Madison. Her poetry appears in *Poets Reading the News, Kissing Dynamite, The Timberline Review, The Ekphrastic Review, Canary: A Literary Journal of the Environmental Crisis, The Poeming Pigeon, Cricket*, and other venues for both adult and young readers. She is a Pushcart Prize nominee and a beginner wildlife photographer. Visit her online at https://elizabethkuelbs.com.

CPSIA information can be obtained
at www.ICGtesting.com
Printed in the USA
LVHW052349021121
702220LV00006B/197